Celtic Mythology

A Guide to Celtic History, Gods, and Mythology

Peter Collins

Table of Contents

Introduction 1

Chapter 1: Who Were the Celts? 6

Chapter 2: Religion of the Celts 20

Chapter 3: Heroes & Monsters in Celtic Mythology 38

Chapter 4: Celtic Magic and Spirituality 58

Chapter 5: Modern Celtic Traditions 73

Conclusion 76

Introduction

We are the fortunate recipients of all the early cultures' recorded history. They left us with mysteries, myths, and folklore to fill our days with intrigue and curiosity. Their accounts have inspired great literature, provided us with an appreciation of a connection with nature, and stimulated many of us to adopt a higher metaphysical meaning to our existence.

Mythology

Mythology comes from many varied cultures that weave sacred tales revolving around gods, heroes, supernatural beings, origin stories, and more. Myths often explain naturally occurring events or how certain customs began within a society. What mythology is to us today was once the religion of yesteryear. Mythology, even if endowed with a questionable amount of magic, was at one time believed to be true. It answers the how, what, where, and why of a civilization.

From prehistoric cave paintings to the written word of scholars such as Homer, myths have provided the human psyche with meaning as they comfort us and explain phenomenon, traditions, geological formations, past events, and supernatural significance.

There are three basic groups that myths can be assigned to:

- Etiological myths typically explain how something came to be or why it is. An example would be the opening of Pandora's box and how evil was introduced into our world.

- Historical myths explain events from the past. For example, in US history, Henry Wadsworth Longfellow created a famous poem based upon the ride of Paul Revere. With the help of Wadsworth's creativity, Revere's ride became epic. In reality, his ride wasn't even mentioned in Revere's obituary. He did not perform the ride alone and was united with other riders that received no tribute or a special story. He did not shout that the British were coming because most of the people living in the area were English.

- Psychological myths usually revolve around a journey from the known to the unknown and a need to balance the world. For example, the explanation of Zeus's anger in Greek mythology is explained away by lightning and thunder.

The Greeks or Romans possess the most well-known myths that enrich their cultures and captivate the student. However, every culture has represented some type of mythology, and often you can find the same or similar story in different cultures.

But there are some cultures that were secretive and did not commit their myths to paper, relying solely on the spoken word handed down from generation to generation. People like the Celts, which is what this book is about, are one of those spoken record keepers. Our knowledge of them can fluctuate, depending upon who is telling the story. In the case of the Celts, many of the records came from the Greeks or the Romans, and since both of them were at one time or another at war with the Celts, we can't help but wonder how accurate those myths might be. Relying on other cultures for explanations can lead to misinformation and misconceptions.

The authors of ancient world myths crafted them on purpose to provide a truth for the reader or audience to interpret.

Folklore

Folklore, on the other hand, is developed from a particular community-based group of people with common traits and a shared identity. Folklore material is shared within the culture to explore traditions, tales, or fine arts. These ideas can be adopted by other cultures and changed as they see fit. A great example is Halloween. What we celebrate today is certainly not comparable to Samhain from the Druids. Yet, there are pieces of tradition in our own Halloween celebrations that have been adopted from the Celts.

For the most part, folklore is shared by repetition, imitation, and observation and often travels beyond the cultural lines. There are some forms, however, that are intended to be understood by only the group that initiated the rituals like the Freemasons and their practices.

Legends

Legends generally begin with an historical fact which undergoes a heavy transformation. The simplest example would be King Arthur. While there is a King Arthur in history, he is not based on the legendary Arthur of legend. Another legend would be of the long sought-after kingdom of Atlantis or the exact location of Avalon.

A legend, even if told from the perspective of history, has no historical background and may resemble a folktale. Included in these legends can be elements of mythology, natural phenomena, or supernatural beings. Often a very old story, legends enjoy popularity even if there is no documentation.

An offshoot of the legend is the urban legend, which is usually a horrifying story that circulates through the population as though true and pops up in multiple locations. Usually, the storyteller of an urban legend alludes to knowing the original people involved or having firsthand knowledge of the story. For example, hookman is found in many rural locations, the tales are usually similar, and they are often perceived as happening to a friend of a friend.

In this book, you will learn all about the mythology, folklore, and history that was specific to the Celts. Let's dive in!

Chapter 1: Who Were the Celts?

The Celts first appeared in recorded history around the sixth century B.C., largely because of trading contracts they had with early Greeks and Phoenicians. By the third century B.C., a large portion of the European continent was controlled by the Celts. This area was north of the Alps mountain range and includes our present-day Ireland and Great Britain.

The Celtic nation covers six locations. They are Scotland, Ireland, Isle of Man, Wales, Cornwall, and Brittany. When we use the word nation, we refer to people who share a common identity and culture.

Before the advancement of Ancient Rome, a large part of Europe was controlled by the Celts.

In truth, the Celts were made up of many people. These tribes throughout the years included the Gaels, Britons, Irish, Picts, Gauls, and Druids. Many languages can be attributed to the Celts. There were originally six confirmed Celtic languages. Four living languages still remain, and they are Breton, Welsh, Irish, and Scottish Gaelic. Two of the languages are extinct, Cornish and Manx.

Breton was brought from Great Britain and is currently spoken in the Brittan region of France. In fact, there are still around thirty-five thousand people who use Breton as their everyday language. Breton has utilized much of the French, Latin, and Gaulish (inactive/extinct) language.

Irish, a known Celtic language, is as you might have guessed, spoken mainly in Ireland. As of a 2016 census, there are still almost two million people in Ireland who speak Irish. The practice of spoken Irish was declining until 1922 when the Irish adopted it as an official language.

Scottish Gaelic is spoken mainly in the Highland and Western Isles but can also be found in the cities of Edinburgh, Inverness, and Glasgow. Although there was a time when children were punished for speaking Gaelic while at school, it is now a subject taught in some schools and universities. Presently, you can even purchase some novels, poetry, and other books written in Gaelic.

Welsh is primarily spoken in Wales, with a couple of scattered colonies found in places like Argentina and Patagonia. There are currently primary schools and secondary schools in Wales that teach using the Welsh language. Along with Scottish Gaelic, Welsh can be found in some areas of England, Canada, Australia, and the USA.

Cornish, although considered somewhat extinct, is still experiencing efforts of a revival. After being rejected by Celtic scholars, Cornish has had a new version recently developed by Dr. Ken George. Currently, there are only around two thousand people who claim to be fluent in the Cornish language, but it is gaining popularity with families who are raising their children using Cornish as their first language. Perhaps we will see a large resurgence of Cornish in years to come.

Manx was spoken solely on the Isle of Man, and the language was declared extinct after the last two native speakers died in the 1960s. However, in the last few decades, there have been some attempts to revive the Manx language. Manx schools have offered Manx classes since the 1990s, and there has been an increase in the creation of songs, stories, novels, and other outlets that showcase the Manx language.

The Tribes of the Celts

Britons

The Britons, also known as Ancient Britons or Celtic Britons, journeyed across the English Channel during the Iron Age, bringing with them their languages and cultures. The territory inhabited by the early Britons was never set in stone, and was constantly changing, therefore exact locations are difficult to pinpoint, but it is generally believed that they inhabited the Island of Great Britain, the kingdoms of Dál Riata, Alba (currently known as Scotland), The Isle of Man, and the channel islands. There were also colonies established in northwestern Spain, Wales, and the northwestern corner of France.

Druids

There is nothing more fascinating than the Celtic society known as the Druids. Because the Druids kept no written record, the group can be often misinterpreted by other cultures from their recorded time. Druids are thought to be from a higher-ranking class of ancient Celtic cultures and probably included medical professionals, lore keepers, and political advisors. Unfortunately, most of the information regarding the Druids is pure speculation. We will never know the full story on Druids because most of their information is left up to interpretation, and different scholars have suggested ties to Siberia, Egypt, and Hindus.

Despite their origins, the Druids influenced many ancient cultures and inspired Eastern traditions. The Druids had ancient historical ties to the Greeks, and Aristotle often referred to their practices and spiritual beliefs. Druids used solar observation areas like Stonehenge to honor their reverence for the sun.

The Druids had extensive knowledge on how to read celestial patterns and an uncanny ability to gauge the seasonal cycles and weather variations. Their festivals such as Beltane also became part of Celtic tradition, which is the day of the arrival of the Tuatha De Danann. The Celtic Druids adopted many spiritual aspects from their predecessors.

The Druid Gods and Goddesses were the Tuatha De Danann, and they came from four cities to the north of Ireland: Falias, Forias, Finias, and Murias. It is said that these ancients acquired their magic and brought with them one magical item from each city. The Tuatha De Danann eventually became the Gods and Goddesses of Celtic Mythology.

It was said that the Tuatha brought with them four magical objects:

- Lia Fáil (The Stone of Fal) - From Falias came the stone of destiny, also known as the Coronation Stone of Tara, and is found on the Hill of Tara in County Meath, Ireland. It is rumored that up until AD 500, all of the kings of Ireland were crowned there. There is some debate and conflicting stories about the origin of the Lia Fáil, but the most popular theory is that the Tuatha De Danann were responsible. The stone was described as magical, and when a rightful King of Ireland put his feet upon it, the stone supposedly roared in joy. It was also rumored that the stone was able to bestow a sort of regeneration upon a king, allowing him to enjoy a long reign.

- The Spear of Lugh is said to have originated from the city of Gorias. Lugh, a member of the Tuatha De Danann, is a prominent god in Irish mythology. Lugh is often described as youthful, large, and handsome. Lugh is described as a master of many disciplines and is linked with a harvest festival called Lughnasadh which is traditionally held on August 1st, which is close to halfway between Summer solstice and Autumn equinox.

- Claíomh Solais (The Sword of Light) - The sword is part of Irish folklore and has a part to play in stories with quests and heroes. Legend says that King Nuada of the Tuatha de Danann brought the sword to Ireland from Finias, and it has been described as a god-slaying weapon. There are many folk tales that spotlight the sword of light.

- Dagda's Cauldron (the cauldron of plenty) - According to legend, the cauldron was made by a Druid called Semias and originated from the city of Murias. The magical power of the caldron allowed it to overflow with a never-ending supply of food. In addition, the caldron was said to have the ability to heal any wound and restore life to the dead.

The Tuatha, according to legend, merged with the land and now exist in the land, stars, bodies of water, planets, and moons.

Druids are a part of Celt heritage even though they ceased to exist somewhere around the fourth century A.D. It is unfortunate that most of the history of the Druids was provided by the written record of the Romans. Julius Caesar in particular was the Roman figure who fabricated tales of brutality and savagery in order to discredit the Druids. The Romans spent a great deal of effort in the elimination of any signs of the Druids because they viewed their philosophy as a threat to the Roman way of life.

The Druid philosophy was in stark contrast to the opinionated religions of the times. They embraced all aspects of total awareness involving the mind, body, and spirit. Members of the Druid order were often advisors for kings, queens, chieftains, and leaders throughout the tribes and clans.

Because the Druids believed that there was nothing fearful about life, they did not acknowledge the concept of good versus evil. Everything was spiritually connected. They believed in metaphysical ideals, the wisdom of nature, and a deeper reality beyond appearances.

They believed in reincarnation, magic, shapeshifting divination, prophecy, a blend of science and spirit, and equal rights for women. Due to the written records of three different civilizations, it can be determined that the Druids did indeed practice some sort of sacrifice. In fact, there is a mostly recovered body from a bog referred to as Lindow Man. Scientists were actually able to recover stomach contents revealing that his last meal was a partially scorched grain cake. Upon examination, it was determined that he was a ritual sacrifice because of showing indications of being strangled, hit on the head, and having his throat cut. The pattern of his injuries is congruent with the written account of 'three-fold' death recorded in medieval Irish tales.

Celtic stories are full of Druids that had the ability to control nature and perform magic. These tales have them wielding wands, communing with tree spirits, and using crystals and gemstones for divination. Mistletoe is actually referred to in Ireland as Druidh lus or Druid's weed. They were strong prophets and the most famous of the Druidic prophets was Merlin.

Gaels

Historians over the centuries have debated the actual origin of the Gaels. It is not known exactly when the Gaels first entered Ireland. The Gaels are one of the Celtic tribal groups that are native to Ireland, Scotland, and the Isle of Man, and their descendants are still found there today. The Gaelic culture and language originated in Ireland and into the west of what is known today as Scotland. Far back in Gael history, it is said that they sailed to Ireland and engaged in a battle of sorcery with the

Tuatha Dé Danann. In folklore, Ériu, a goddess of the land, promises that in exchange for tribute to her, the Gaels shall be welcomed in Ireland. It is conjectured that this is when the Tuath Dé Danann traveled to the world below, or the Otherworld, while the Gaels took the world above.

The Otherworld in Celtic mythology is a world of the gods, and it may possibly include the world of the dead.

The Gaels were the last Celtic tribe to migrate to Ireland, but they brought their language and organization to the people.

After the early seventeenth century, the Gaels fit into a clan which was a large group of related people that all descended from one male chieftain or king. Even though the clans were based on blood relations, they also accepted others into the group for various reasons. Warfare between clans was common during these times.

Their religion was usually pagan, and they believed in many gods and goddesses. Religious practices were taught to all Gaels, and these traditions were passed down through the generations by only the spoken word.

Like the Egyptians, the Gaels have been found to be buried with food, weapons, and other items that might be needed in the afterlife. Animals have been found to be significant to the Gaels during archaeological digs and have also turned up in many of their stories.

Early Gaels had faith in magic, divine life, and magical entities such as leprechauns and faeries. They celebrated four pagan festivals each year: Imbolic, Bealtaine, Lughnasadn, and Samhain. With the coming of Christianity to Ireland, the monks adopted the Gaels myths to fit the Christian traditions.

Gauls

The Gauls were Celtic people originating during the Iron Age in Europe. By the fourth century B.C., the Gauls had spread out over a large region that encompasses present day France, Belgium, the Netherlands, Switzerland, Southern Germany, Austria, Slovakia, and the Czech Republic. Reaching their pinnacle of power sometime in the third century B.C., the Gauls were eventually taken over by the Romans and Julius Caesar after many years of the Gallic Wars. Over time, the Gauls combined their culture with others, and the end result was a group of Celtic people that make up modern France.

The Gauls, much like the Gaels, buried their dead with cherished items like weapons and chariots, showing reverence for someone who had passed on. Excavations have revealed that some bodies were laid to rest inside a stone casing built into the ground. A large slab carved from stone was placed on top to cover the body's final resting place.

During their war with the Romans, the Gauls engaged in a particularly brutal practice of removing the heads from their enemies. A recent excavation of Gallic burials resulted in the discovery of eleven embalmed heads that were decapitated and kept. The methods used to preserve the heads are currently unknown, but it is believed that they flaunted their conquests by displaying the heads publicly. All Gaul bodies on record have been buried sitting upright and facing north.

The Gauls were strong, warrior-like people who provided many holidays that we still practice today. The Gauls did not disappear but evolved into others within the Celtic culture including the Druids.

Irish

It was generally believed that the Celts arrived in the area now known as Ireland around 500 B.C., but Irish scholars no longer support this theory. Irish archaeologists looked for evidence to support this date and the stories but could find no real evidence to support the lore. Unfortunately, because of the Celts aversion to the written word, we can only go by what has been recorded since the arrival of Christianity. This date was first arrived at by an Irish document called the Book of Invasions, but this was conceived over a thousand years after the event, and it is unknown how accurate these accounts were. Within this document are great Irish tales with tantalizing descriptions of gods and goddesses, along with the supernatural order of the Druids. This account of Irish mythology portrays heroes, heroines, warriors, and the wars they fought.

The Book of Invasions portrays the original people of Ireland as the mythical Fir Bolg people who developed Ireland into provinces. Following the Fir Bolg came the Túatha Dé Danann who were skilled at magic, and according to the tale, defeated the Fir Bolg in battle, allowing them to take over the country.

Mythology proclaims that the Gaels arrived and claimed the land, defeating the Túatha Dé Danann who moved to reside in the Otherworld. On their journey to Tara, the pinnacle place of worship in Ireland, the Gaels met the goddess Ériu, who foretold them that Ireland would belong to them for all time.

Interestingly, archaeologists have been unable to find evidence to support the idea of a mass migration to the shores of Ireland. There was neither evidence of lifestyle changes nor burial styles to support the theories. There have never been Celtic type burial chambers found in Ireland.

Despite the lack of archaeological evidence, the Celtic language and culture did arrive in Ireland. Could it have occurred because of migration that was spread out over a large amount of time? It stands to reason that whole families would have migrated to Ireland instead of just warriors. It would require the influence of women and families to pass on the Celtic language and speech to the country. Scholars are divided to this day upon how, when, or if the Celtic people journeyed to Ireland. Because of the Celts tradition of oral history, sadly, no one will ever know for sure.

Picts

The Picts lived in what we know of today as the northern and eastern parts of Scotland. Just like the rest of the Celts, the Picts kept no early written records, but they are believed to be the descendants of the Caledonians, a Brittonic tribe from the Iron Age. At some point prior to the year nine hundred, it is believed that the Picts merged with the Gaelic kingdom. Picts were often referred to as painted people because of their custom of tattooing their bodies and their use of warpaint.

Even though there were many years of warring with the Romans, the Picts were able to hold their territory and never fell under the invading Romans. Under similar circumstances to the Irish, there is no Pictish invasion mentioned in history. It is generally believed that they had always been there. They were farmers and fishermen, but all were warriors underneath. The Picts appeared to live peacefully unless they were menaced by an outside force like the Romans. Although the Romans won battles, they never succeeded in overtaking Scotland.

During the time that Columba was spreading Christianity, the Pictish developed a stronghold in the area of Inverness. In an account by St. Adamnan on St. Columba, there is included a legend of a large monster who existed beneath the waters of the River Ness. He related a tale of the monster eating inhabitants of the region around the time of Columba's arrival. The story goes on to say that Columba saved one of his traveling companions from the monster's attack by invoking the name of God. In doing so, he terrified the creature and it fled. The defeat of the monster was supposedly the turning point for the Picts, who were so impressed by Columba's feat that they converted to Christianity. One has to wonder if this tale was the basis for all the following stories regarding the Loch Ness Monster.

Pictish people were able to use advanced architectural principles, create great art, possessed skills in navigation, and were highly skilled craftsmen.

Did the Picts disappear from history? Apparently not! Recent DNA evidence shows that ten percent of Scottish men are descended from the Picts. It is generally believed that the Picts and the Scots may have banded together against a common enemy, and the people merely intermingled. With no written records, one can only theorize on the disappearance of the Picts.

Chapter 2: Religion of the Celts

The Romans described the Celts as religious people, but they also viewed them as barbaric and alien. With no actual written records, again we must rely on opinions from other cultures. The Greeks and Romans have muddied the waters while attempting to equate the Celtic gods with their own.

The Celtic religion believed in a moral system distinguishing right from wrong. There were beliefs taught to the people guiding them as to what was lawful or unlawful, and afterward self-salvation was up to the individual. The Celts believed that men and women possessed their own free will and were responsible for their own actions.

Still, there are some things about the Celtic religion that can be observed. For one thing, we know that they believed in and worshipped more than one god. There are over some four hundred names of Celtic gods, but many of them are only represented locally, leaving almost a hundred that were the major players in the deity pool of the Celts.

Archeological evidence even today has very little to offer in regard to the priests who officiated at Celtic religious ceremonies. There have been several artifacts found such as crowns, headdresses, metal face masks, and hand-held objects.

It is surmised that there may have been moments during rituals when the priest's face had to be hidden or a time when it might be forbidden to look upon a priest's face.

Another religious Celtic custom was called a ritual shaft. The Celts would dig pits and shafts down into the ground, which are speculated to have been used in reaching down into the Underworld in the attempt to connect both worlds. This custom was used across the entire Celtic world and became extended into the Greco-Roman world. At a place called Holzhausen, there was a site found that contained three shafts described as ritual shafts. One of these three contained evidence of animal or human sacrifice. These pits could also have been used for grain storage or an attempt to construct a holy well. The Romans provided writings stating that the Celts would cover their altars with the blood of their captives and used human entrails to commune with their gods. One account of an Iron Age shaft found in Bavaria contained a post at the bottom that tested positive for human blood. It is assumed that this was used to impale human victims. Examples such as these perpetuate the myths of sacrifices made to Otherworld dwelling deities.

There is a twelfth century source that states that the Ancient Irish used to offer the firstborn child of each family to their stone idol, Mag Slocht. Since the Druids were a religious social class of the Celts, it would be reasonable to assume that they would have also participated in, and likely officiated, at human sacrifices. If one believes the Roman reports, they claim that when the Celts ran out of prisoners and criminals, they drew from the innocent populace. It has also been reported that among the human bones were found those of dogs. There are difficult questions surrounding these various reports because if this is true, where are all the bodies? Since we only have Roman propaganda stories to draw conclusions with, we will most likely never be able to provide a definitive answer to this question.

Did the Celts practice ritualistic sacrifices? Even though there are no official records from the Celts themselves, other civilizations wrote about their practices. Evidence has also been found suggesting that they did, and it was the belief that the Celts ritually sacrificed their kings in an attempt to appease their gods. Some bodies recovered in an Ireland bog prove that not only were they sacrificed, but they endured horrible deaths if their reign took a bad turn. The bodies showed evidence of ritual torture.

The Celtic deities were revered and often referred to as a triple or triune deity. Whether they had three names, three faces, three heads, or were depicted as three sisters, the Druids always taught the sacred number of three. The Celts carried on in the tradition of the three with pre-Roman coins depicting a three headed deity. Ireland had a female triple goddess (sisters) with the given names of Éore, Bamba, and Fótla.

You can find throughout the Celts religion the example of body, soul, and spirit, or how they divided the earth into earth, sea, and air. Do these sound familiar? How about animal, vegetable, or mineral, or our cardinal colors of yellow, red, blue? These are all triunes from the Celts. Even in Christian churches today we have the Father, Son, and the Holy Ghost, most likely adapted from the ancient Celts.

Celts believed that the soul resided in the head, and they recognized it as the source of power. Perhaps that is why they chose to take the heads of their enemies after they fell in battle? It has been suggested that by keeping the head of their enemy, the Celts controlled their spirit.

Traditional myths mention the importance of the head and how the owner was able to live on once separated from the dead body. For example, in Celtic myth, there lived a giant Celtic deity named Bran Bendigeidfran. According to the Welsh account, he was mortally wounded by poison. The description of this event goes on to say that he ordered his men to cut off his head before the poison reached it with orders to take his head back to Britain. The myth states that the severed head talked, joked, and gave advice to them the entire journey.

The afterlife was important to the Celtic religion. They had faith that the soul was immortal and would reincarnate. Depending upon previous actions, the Celts believed that a soul would reincarnate in human, animal, or plant form. Death was only the beginning, and the soul would change places and travel to the world of the dead or the Otherworld. When a soul died in the Otherworld, they would return to this one.

The Celts often buried grave goods of personal belongings, weapons, and food and drink in order to give the dead a good start in the Otherworld.

Otherworld

Celtic myths suggest that their deities and the faerie people lived in a domain called the Otherworld. No mortal eyes were able to see this realm because it was hidden by magic and was considered by the Celts to be their version of heaven. Otherworld was often referred to as Sidhe, Annwfn, or Annwyn.

The passage of time in Otherworld is unlike our concept of time. What may only be a year in the Otherworld can be centuries in our own. Celtic literature provides many stories filled with journeys to Otherworld. One of the most well-known of the Celtic journeys was that of Oísin who rode off on a magical horse and remained in the Otherworld for three hundred years. While in Otherworld, he was enthralled by a daughter of the king of the Otherworld and forced to marry her. One day, she allowed him to return briefly to the mortal world with the understanding that he may not set foot on land. Throughout his adventure back in the mortal world, he stopped to help several men from the land. When he did so, his saddle girth snapped and he touched the ground for only a second, but that was all that was needed. Before the other's eyes, Oísin aged rapidly until he crumbled to dust and blew away in the wind.

Only one day of the year was the Otherworld visible to the mortal world, and that day was during the feast of Samhain on October thirty-first to November first. During this time, it was explained that the supernatural veil between worlds broke down and both the living and the dead could wander freely between the lands. Lore states that those tormented or killed by the living could return to haunt them. Christianity made every attempt to suppress their belief in Samhain but finally adopted it with some variations, making November first All Hallows Day and the evening before became known as Halloween.

Irish Celtic myth stated that there were two deities whose sole purpose was to escort souls to the Otherworld.

Gods & Goddesses

Celtic mythology stories are filled with stories of many Gods and Goddesses. However, there are problems identifying the deities worshipped by the Celts. The information is not always clear and often it is difficult to discern if there are many gods or several manifestations of one god. Since the Celtic world was broken up into different tribes, it is easy to guess that they might have local gods. We may never have an absolute description of these gods and goddesses since they were Romanized. Nevertheless, let's take a look at some of the more well-known ones and provide you with some details of each.

Airmid/Airmed - Goddess of Witchcraft & Lore

Airmid is a healing goddess of the Tuatha Dé Danann and keeper of Spring. She was prayed to for aiding in magic, healing, herbalism, and bringing the dead back to life.

Aonghus/Aengus - God of Love & Youth

The son of Boanna and Dagda. The story of Aonghus says that he searched all of Ireland for a beautiful young woman, and after a long search, he found one named Caer. She was one of a hundred and fifty young maidens who were to be turned into swans during the feast of Samhain. It is said that Aonghus transformed himself into a swan so that he would remain with Caer.

Arawn - God of the Underworld

The Welsh lord of the Otherworld, Arawn is portrayed as a fair and honorable ruler. He is also known as a powerful hunter and magician. It was rumored that every day, he went hunting with his court members and his supernatural white-eared, red-eyed, dogs. With the traditional Celtic year ending on the holiday of Samhain, and that day being set aside for the dead to walk freely on earth, it was a popular time for the Lord of the Underworld.

With the arrival of the Christians however, he was given negative traits that he never possessed, and became Lord of the Damned, watching over all who were barred from the Christian paradise and setting his hellhounds loose to hunt for the souls of the unclean.

Arawn can still be found today in some very unusual places. For example, in the role-playing game, Dungeons & Dragons, Arawn plays the Celtic Lord of the Underworld!

Belenus/Belenos/Bel/Beli Mawr - The Sun God

Belenus was often depicted as riding across the sky in his horse drawn chariot or riding astride his horse. Either way, he was known to throw thunderbolts on his journeys. The Romans instantly identified their own god, Apollo, with Belenus.

Described as one of the more powerful gods, Belenus was also associated with the power to heal and regenerate. The strength and legacy of Belenus continues to this day through the festival of Beltane. This celebration was originally observed to signify the healing powers of the spring sun.

Boanna - The Goddess of the River

Depending upon which text you read, Boanna's husbands tended to change. Some pair her with Nechtan (a mortal), Elemar, Uaithne, or Dagda. Boanna is credited with poetry, flowing water, spiritual insight, fertility, knowledge, and creativity. She is able to clear your mind of negativity and helps open your soul to receive inspiration.

Brigid - Goddess of Healers, Poets, Smiths, Childbirth, and Inspiration - Also the Goddess of Fire and Hearth - Patron of Warfare

Also known as Brigantia, Brid, Bride, Briginda, Brigdu, and Brigit, she is now also remembered in Christianity as St. Brigit or St. Bride. There is a festival that honors her known as Imbolc that is held every February first and is said to usher in springtime. In Ireland, they make a bride's cross which has often been described as an ancient solar symbol.

Brigid was even honored in a Druidic ritual consisting of a well containing candles. The well was adorned with flowers and greens, and often coins and other objects made of silver were deposited in the well as an offering. Yet another tradition to honor Brigid is for villagers to leave a loaf of bread, pitcher of milk, and a candle out for the goddess.

Cernunnos - The Horned One

Connected to wild animals, fertility, and wealth, Cernunnos is depicted as having the antlers of a stag atop his head. Cernunnos is sometimes a catchall for horned gods of nature since not all of them are named. Cernunnos is the god of the forest, nature, fertility, fruit, corn, beasts, and human prosperity, and while important as a Gaulish deity, Cernunnos was not adopted by the Romans. He is often depicted with a stag, boar, bull, and ram-horned snake, and some have conjectured that his close association with the stag implies the ability to shapeshift. Even though Cernunnos was benevolent, the Christians only saw a horned god which to them meant the Devil.

Crom Cruach - The Lord of the Mound

Found in Irish folklore, Chrome Cruach was said to have had bloody rituals dedicated to him by eleventh century monks.

Dagda - The Good God

Described as having unparalleled strength and appetite, Dagda is known as the Irish father of all the gods. He carried a large club that possessed the power to kill men as well as bring them back to life. Dagda is often pictured as a club-wielding giant who owns a magic caldron that is never empty. Unlike other godlike contemporaries, Dagda is often described as ugly, rough, and crude, but still treated as a figure of fun that has a propensity to crave porridge and play the harp. According to some reports, he was married to the goddess Boanna.

Danu - Matriarch of Power/Mother Goddess

Mother goddess of the Tuatha Dé Danann, all other gods are said to be descended from her. An ancient deity, Danu has remained a mystery but was said to grant gifts to rulers and those born of noblemen. Described as the mother of gods, Danu is recognized as the central goddess. Danu has also been called the goddess of earth, fertility, wind, wisdom, and has a connection with faeries and faerie lore.

The mother goddess is complicated to describe. She is depicted by bringing together the living and the dead, yet effigies of her are buried in tombs with the corpses. For reasons unknown, she is often associated with warfare.

Epona - Goddess of the Horse

Epona was one of the few gods or goddesses chosen to be adopted by the Romans. She is not only the goddess of horses, but she is also associated with a cornucopia, fertility, and accompanying the soul on its final journey.

Many of her worshippers were soldiers or cavalrymen. She is almost always depicted as riding sidesaddle on a horse or surrounded by horses. Epona was most likely also the patron saint of horse breeding and is generally regarded as the protector of horsemen.

Ériu/Eire - The Goddess of Ireland, Banba - Patron Goddess of Ireland, and Fódla - Giantess of Ireland

This trio of sisters are known as Tuatha Dé Danann. Ériu has the honor of having the entire nation of Ireland named after her. Fódla and Banba are sometimes used as literary names for Ireland. All three sisters asked for their names to be used for Ireland, but Ériu was granted the primary name use for the country.

Esus

Very little is known about this god, but two stone reliefs carved for him depict him as a woodcutter. There have been interpretations that name him a god of vegetation. There have been some theories that early rituals to ensure fertility contained early ritual human or animal tributes, but there is no evidence that he was worshipped with human sacrifices.

Grannus - God of Healing

Grannus may have been associated with the sun, thermal springs, or spas. Again, Grannus has been subjected to Roman intervention, but he is often associated with healing springs.

Lugh/Lugus/Lug - The Courageous Warrior God

Lugh was often described as a youthful, handsome warrior and more sophisticated than Dagda. Lugh was known to carry a spear and had the ability to defeat evil beings from the Otherworld.

Often accompanied by thunderstorms, ravens, and lynxes, Lugh was thought to be able to kill from any distance which most likely would mean that his power was long reaching.

This powerful Celtic god was thought of by the Romans as Mercury.

Mannannán Mac Lir/Manawydan - Irish Sea God

One of his powers was the ability to create illusion, and with it, he carried heroes to the Otherworld across the sea or beneath it. His name translates as 'son of the sea,' and he has connections to the waters off the coast of Ireland and the Isle of Man.

He is known to possess a magical horse called Aonbarr and a magical sword called The Answerer. In a famous tale from Irish Literature, he is featured in The Voyage of Bran where he is described as traveling across the sea in his horse drawn chariot.

Morrigan - Goddess of War

Her name supposedly means 'great queen,' 'phantom queen,' or 'queen of the demons.' It was generally believed that she took the form of a crow or raven, and while flying over a given battlefield, she was supposed to be able to influence or predict a battle's outcome. It is said that she brings death, destruction, and chaos. Though she never partakes in the battle, it is said that she uses magic to generate terror between the rival warriors.

Nantosuelta - The Domestic Goddess/Goddess of Nature, Earth, Fire & Fertility

This goddess is often depicted carrying a model of a house on the end of a long pole. Her name translates to Winding River.

She is often shown with her companion, Sucellus, the hammer god. In addition to his hammer, he can also be seen carrying a bowl or pot referencing anything from beer or wine to honey.

Nehalennia - unknown goddess

Accompanied almost always by a wolfhound, this Roman/Celtic Goddess is a subject of debate among scholars. Some believe her to be the goddess of merchants because there is often a basket at her feet filled with apples or other fruits, or her feet are shown to be on the bow of a ship. Other scholars believe that she stands for darker reasons and connects her to the role of goddess of the dead. The dog at her feet can be interpreted with either healing, or with the Underworld.

Regardless of her vocation, inscriptions and altars have been found that were dedicated to her. Her temple, once covered by ocean waters, was unearthed off the coast of Zeeland in the year 1645 enabling archaeologists to rediscover her secrets.

Ogmios/Ogma - the God of Eloquence/Lord of Knowledge

Visually, Ogmios was depicted as wearing lion skins, carrying clubs and bows, and having long chains made of amber and gold attached to his tongue. Believed to be a son of Dagda, this god was given credit to the invention of the earliest writing system in Ireland.

He was a champion of the Tuatha Dé Danann and was said to have crafted curse tablets. A curse tablet is a binding spell that has many meanings. They are said to ask the gods different things or be used for magical influence. There were not always negative connotations tied to the curse tablets, because often they were used to help the dead and lay their souls to rest.

Rhiannon - Great Queen

Since Rhiannon has been linked closely with horses, it has been suggested that she and Epona may be the same. Appearing in Welsh hero-legends, Rhiannon is shown as a beautiful woman with a long flowing robe, riding a white horse. In addition, she is also linked with birds, and both horses and birds are considered to be symbolic of the Underworld.

Entwined in a Celtic story, Rhiannon is accused of killing and eating her infant child and condemned to tell her story to every stranger that passes her way in addition to carrying them upon her back. Eventually, according to legend, she is changed into a horse.

Taranis - The God of Thunder

Taranis is conjectured to be in the ancient triad of Celtic gods consisting of Esus, Toutatis, and Taranis. The Romans compared him to their god, Jupiter (and the Greek god Zeus) with the resemblance of hurling lightning bolts. However, Taranis was also portrayed with a solar wheel and is connected to fire in the sky.

Like most of the Celtic gods, there is little known about him, but he was said to travel across the skies at high speed. If one believes the Roman writings of Julius Caesar, he was a god that human sacrifices were made to by being burned inside of a 'wicker man.'

There are some writings by Lucan about a dangerous cult of Taranis that practiced human sacrifices. Supposedly, sizable figures were fashioned made of wicker and filled with human victims made up of thieves or other criminals and set ablaze. In fact, archaeologists have discovered thousands of votive wheels that they believe tie into the cult of Taranis.

Toutatis/Teutates/Tuathal Techtmar - The Guardian God of Gauls

While not much is known about this powerful Celtic god, Toutatis was thought of as important because his name roughly translates to 'God of the People.' This made him a guardian or tribal protector.

The Romans mentioned Toutatis/Teutates as one of the three major gods of the Celts, and they described him as cruel.

Chapter 3: Heroes & Monsters in Celtic Mythology

Every culture is full of stories to uplift and entertain, and the Celts were no different. Below you will find some of the more popular stories from Celtic mythology, detailing the adventures of heroes, monsters, and more!

Heroes & Myths

Ballad of Bran

During the tenth century on the coast of Leon, the Bretons marched to repel the raiding Norsemen. Though the Norsemen were repelled, they still managed to capture and carry off some prisoners, including a wounded warrior called Bran.

Bran wept at his misfortune, and when the Norsemen reached their home shore, he was imprisoned in a tower. He finally convinced his jailors to allow him to send a letter to his mother. Bran advised the messenger to dress as a beggar in order to stay safe, and along with the message, Bran sent his gold ring so his mother would know the message was real.

Bran told the messenger to go directly to his mother, and if she will pay my ransom, you must fly a white sail, but if she refuses you must fly a black sail.

When the message was delivered and read, Bran's mother sailed immediately to retrieve her son.

When Bran questioned his guard about a ship with a sail, the guard lied to the young man and told him the sail was black. Bran, overwhelmed by despair, died.

When his mother arrived, she demanded to see the body of her son. Once the door was opened, she threw herself down on her son's body, and she too died of despair.

On the site of the battle between the Bretons and the Norsemen, an oak tree marks the spot where the Norsemen retreated. At night, birds gather on the oak to sing, except for a gray rook and a young crow.

It is said that the crow speaks and says, "Sing, little birds, sing. When you die you will at least end your days in Brittany." The crow is believed to be Bran, and the rook, his mother.

Breton tradition states that the dead may return to earth in the form of birds.

Cuchullain

Cuchullain is a famous Irish Hero and is known to be one of the oldest stories. Part of the Ulster Cycle, the tales were preserved in a work called The Cattle Raid of Cooley, which is considered a great Irish epic. In this tale we are taken to an invasion of Ulster by Queen Mebd.

According to the legend, Cuchullain, who was a son of the god Lugh, was impervious to a curse that paralyzed all others, both regular men and heroes. This left him as the only one to fight off the invaders.

It was rumored that Cuchullain could be driven into a rage where his skin was said to turn red from heat and his face would shift into that of a monster. When the battle was over, his comrades were said to pour water over him to cool down his rage.

Fionn Mac Cumhail or Finn McCool

Cumhaill was born a giant and was the son of a leader of a band of warriors called the Fianna. When Benandonner, another giant from Scotland, threatened Ireland, Fionn is said to have retaliated by tearing up chunks of the coastline and hurling them into the sea. By doing this, Fionn created a walkway that allowed him to travel across the sea to reach Benandonner. Unfortunately, Fionn finds himself outmatched and retreats to

Ireland, disguised as a baby. After Benandonner arrives in Ireland, he sees Fionn as a baby, and believing him to truly be just a regular baby, he is worried about how large the father must be. Following this line of thinking, Benandonner makes great haste to return to Scotland and begins to tear up as much of the walkway as possible. Herein lies the myth of how the Giant's Causeway was created.

The Dullahan

In mythology, the Dullahan is always seen as a headless rider astride a black horse, and underneath his arm, he carried his head. Although supposedly male, there have been some female versions of this myth born from Ireland.

The head is described as wearing a horrifying grin that reaches both sides of the head, and the eyes are said to be in constant motion to see the countryside. The flesh is portrayed to have the color and texture of moldy cheese. The whip of the headless rider is believed to be the spine of a human corpse. The ancient Irish were of the belief that the spot where the Dullahan stopped his ride was where a person would soon die. If the Dullahan calls out a person's name, he is able to draw away the soul of his victim where the person drops dead.

The Each-Uisge

Called a water horse, the Each-Uisge can be found in the Scottish Highlands. While it bears a resemblance to the Kelpie of the fae, the Each-Uisge is considered to be more dangerous and vicious.

Living in the sea and lochs, the Each-Uisge is a talented shapeshifter that appears to its prey as a fine horse, pony, or handsome man. While in horse form, should a man mount it to ride, the rider is only safe while away from the water. At the smallest hint of water, the rider is doomed because the Each-Uisge's skin becomes glue-like, trapping the rider. The creature heads for the deepest part of the nearest loch with its victim, and after he has drowned his rider, he tears him apart and devours everything except for the liver.

Arthur

No journey into the land of the Celts would be complete without looking at the legend of King Arthur.

The legend of Arthur reveals that although born of adultery, he became one the most celebrated rulers of Britain. He is said to have led his Knights of the Round Table on daring adventures where they faced and killed witches, giants, and monsters, causing the people to unite behind the warrior king.

Arthur was conceived by trickery when King Uther Pendragon of the round table masqueraded himself to be the Duke of Cornwall and tricked his way into the bed of Ingraine, the Duke's wife. This deceit culminated in the conception of Arthur. When the child was born, he was taken away to be raised by the wizard Merlin. According to the legend, it was Merlin himself who had arranged for Uther to be in charge of the one hundred and fifty knights that sat at the round table. When Uther died, there was no heir, and the knights were unsure as to who the successor would be. Merlin tells the knights that whoever pulls the sword from the stone should be the next king. It is said that many tried, but none succeeded. A day arrived when Arthur was serving as a squire for his foster brother Sir Kay and was sent to replace a broken sword. Passing Excalibur encased in stone, Arthur drew it out, unaware of the legend. This action proclaimed him to be the new king!

Uniting Britain, Arthur is responsible for driving off the Saxons, and he becomes a king of the people. During his reign, he became known for his heroic deeds, including the legendary quest for the Holy Grail. Though King Arthur was not responsible for finding the cup of Christ, his knight, Sir Galahad was.

Despite the warnings of Merlin, King Arthur marries Lady Guinevere, the daughter of the King of Scotland. But, Guinevere loves another and the affair between her and Sir Lancelot results in Lancelot fleeing for France with Arthur in pursuit. During Arthur's absence, his nephew Mordred is said to have taken the throne which ended with a battle upon Arthur's return. During the battle, most of the knights ended up dying, and Arthur himself was seriously wounded. The tale ends with Arthur abandoning Excalibur at the bottom of a lake when he boarded a boat destined for the magical Isle of Avalon. He leaves, hoping to be cured of his wounds so that one day he can return and lead his people.

One of the main mysteries in the King Arthur legend is the location of the fabled Camelot. It is believed that Camelot was not one single place, but several locations. Another mystery is the location of Avalon. Could this be a name for the Underworld? If it is a magical place where King Arthur was taken to die or be healed, then where is the location? There is no actual answer as to whether Arthur died on the battlefield or whether he was rescued or wounded. The likeliest location of Arthur's final battle is somewhere on the Eden River, somewhere in North Wales. If he was indeed rescued, the safest route would have taken the rescue party west into the Irish Sea, but where did they go after that? Choices include Bardsley Island, The Isle of Man, a supernatural island called Emhain Abhlach, or a spot on the Scottish shore once called Ynys Afallach, which translates to "The Island of the Lord of the Dead."

Stories of a sleeping king entombed in a cave or on an island were told prior to the Arthurian Celtic beliefs. Is Arthur's repose in

Avalon a sort of suspended animation where he lies still close to death but capable of being recalled to life?

So, was King Arthur real? The debate has gone on for centuries and will most likely continue. Whether King Arthur was a real king, a hero of lore, or even a long-lost Celtic deity, his legacy continues to inspire writers, painters, dreamers, and filmmakers to produce their own version of the legend.

Fae

Within many cultures reside the tales of beings that have supernatural and magical abilities. Even though these beings may share human characteristics, they can be dangerous and frightening or playful and benevolent depending upon their mood. The current description of a faerie is a being with human form but having magical powers. Faeries have been called many names over the years, but some of the more common are: Brownie, Elemental, Nature Spirit, Naiad, Pooka, Selkie, Sidhe, and Wee Folk.

There are some common threads of stories revolving around the Fae within the Celtic nations. They are usually described as a mythical group or race who have been forced into hiding because of an invader.

The very nature of a faerie is to be mischievous and spiteful, however, there were some faeries who gave protection, provided healing, or gave skills to a mortal. Depending upon the culture, the faeries could be described as anything from playful to malicious.

The belief and influence of the faerie race became more prevalent when the ancient people changed from hunters to farmers. Even though the faeries are linked to the Druids, it is believed that they are much older and are more prolific in Ireland and Scotland than in Britain.

The Celts believed the fae to be the agricultural gods and goddesses of the earth, holding control over the growth of crops and the yield they provided. Because of this, the Celts often provided offerings of milk, honey, and other foods to the fae.

The fae are considered a sacred earth spirit that brightens nature. The Sidhe are considered the land faeries, and the water faeries are called Merrows. The Merrows are believed to bring bad weather and march from the sea in either the shape of humans with fish tails, or hornless cows.

According to the Celts, pagan deities often transformed into faeries. A famous example might be the Lady of the Lake, the mysterious woman who handed King Arthur his sword.

The Celts were positive that the faeries were capable of being invisible and always nearby so they could listen without being seen. For that reason, they believed that it was always prudent to speak well of them. In Celtic Culture, faeries were very active and had the ability to travel great distances.

It is difficult to pinpoint exactly where faerie lore originated from, but the belief in the fae is part of a pagan, pre-Christian world. In the post-Christian times, faeries were often referred to as fallen angels or elemental spirits. During the seventeenth century, people viewed faeries as darker beings with evil in their hearts.

The faeries are rumored to have Otherworld palaces and kingdoms where they are said to hold festivals, battle with neighboring tribes, and play music. It is thought that they can travel through the thinner veils on the eve of the great feasts like Beltane or Samhain and walk among the mortal world.

If a mortal being travels to the faerie realm, they must take care to never eat or drink because if they do, they will be trapped in the realm and would never be allowed to return home. Others believe if you consume their food you will be gifted with having the ability to see the fae.

Have you ever witnessed a dark circle of green within a lighter green lawn? That is what the Celtic people believed to be a faerie ring or portal to their realm. A faerie ring can also be made up of a circle of mushrooms, and other portals can be found at the base of an old tree, a cave, an opening in the ground, or a ring of crystals. It is understood that one should not interfere with any portal to the faerie realm and should only enter them if you know what you are doing.

There are certain times that the veils are thinner between the realms. As we mentioned before, there is Beltane and Samhain, but also the other eight great days:

- Yule, winter solstice
- Bridget's Fire, (February second)
- Hertha's Day, spring equinox
- Beltane, (May first)
- Letha's Day, summer solstice
- Lughnassad, (first week of August)
- Hellith's Day, autumnal equinox
- Samhain, (October thirty-first)

In addition, the veils are thinnest at the thirteen full moons:

- Wolf Moon
- Storm Moon
- Chaste Moon
- Seed Moon
- Hare Moon
- Dyad Moon
- Mead Moon

- Wort Moon
- Barley Moon
- Wine Moon
- Blood Moon
- Snow Moon
- Oak Moon

Walking through a fae portal can cause change and personal transformation. It is believed that while in their realm there is no death, no aging, no sickness, and no ugliness.

There are rumored to be many types of faeries, some are well known to humans and others remain invisible and hidden.

Alven

These water faeries are from the Netherlands and are found in ponds. Unlike traditional fae, the Alven have no wings, but are able to fly by being encased in a bubble and traveling with the wind. It is rumored that they can shapeshift into otters.

Ashrays

These are also known as water faeries, but they reign from Scotland and appear to look like a twenty-something human, either male or female. Because they are white and nocturnal, these faeries are often mistaken for a ghost at sea. It is alleged that if sunlight should hit them, they will melt into a rainbow-colored pond.

Asrai

The Asrai are tiny and frail female faeries. Like the Ashrays, they cannot be exposed to sunshine or they melt away.

Ballybog

These ancient Irish faeries guard the peat bogs of Ireland. They appear very ugly and are covered from head to toe in mud.

Banshee

The Banshee are rumored to warn of a coming death to the families that they are connected to. They are known for shrieking loudly but are described as looking different in different regions. She can be dressed in white or resemble a green hag with unkempt hair and long nails.

Brownies

Brownies are known to be friendly and helpful with human families. They are an earthen faerie and pick a house or garden with a nice family to help out with chores and care of the garden.

Changeling

This is an ugly faerie that is put in the place of a human child stolen by the fae.

Dryads

A faerie creature known to the Druids that dwells in oak trees.

Elves

These are faeries from Scottish folklore that are split into the Seelie (mildly dangerous) and Unseelie (malicious) courts of the fae.

Gwragedd Annwn

These are Welsh faeries who tend to choose human men as their husbands.

Gwyllion

These are Scottish water faeries described as extremely hairy males who ambush lost travelers on dark mountain roads.

Heather Pixie

This pixie faerie is described as having delicate features and translucent wings. A native of Scotland and England, they love the moors and the heather that grows around them.

Irish Sea Water Guardians

This faerie was said to originate in the Isle of Man. These small faeries are said to be surrounded by a greenish blue light and guard the Irish seas. For some reason, they are supposed to be extremely active during sea storms.

Kelpie

This faerie is described as a shape-shifting water horse seen in Scotland and Ireland. Kelpies are said to lure their meals from the shoreline, and that can include deer, other faeries, and even humans. Accounts say that the male kelpies can shapeshift into handsome men to lure young women into the water where they consume them.

Moura Encantada

Described as charming and beautiful, these faeries often are depicted as singing and combing long red hair with their golden combs. These faeries are said to be able to shapeshift and can be dangerous.

Pixies

These are naughty faeries that love a good practical joke, and they don't care if the victim of the prank is human or another faerie. Pixies love to steal horses to ride and make their home in flower gardens.

Selkie

The Selkie is a known shapeshifter and even though it is a water faerie it can appear as a seal or a human.

Celtic Creatures A-Z

Celtic folklore has several legendary creatures that have graced their history. We have compiled some of the most noteworthy into the list below:

- Abhartach - One of the neamh-mairbh or walking dead. Legend has it that he can only be killed with a sword made of yew wood, then he must be buried upside down, and then his grave must be surrounded with thorns. Then the grave must be topped off by placing a large stone on top.

- Balor - A giant and the king of the Fomarians.

- Bánánach - From early Irish folklore and best described as a ghost that haunts battlefields.

- Baobhan Sith - Said to be a female vampire that haunts the highland regions.

- Baisd Bheulach - Depicted as a shapeshifting demon who haunts the Odail Pass on the Isle of Skye. It is said that its howls can be heard all through the night.

- Bean Nighe - In Scottish folklore, she is regarded as an omen of death from the Otherworld.

- Black Annis - Is described as a tall hag with a blue face and iron claws. She is a cannibal that lives in a cave in the Dane Hills located in Leicestershire, England. She is said to hide in an oak tree so that she may leap on children and lambs to devour them. Supposedly, the Black Annis grinds her teeth which produces a noise alerting her prey.

- Bodach - Best known in Scottish folklore as a being that comes down the chimney and kidnaps naughty children.

- Boobrie - A giant black bird that sports webbed feet and reportedly feeds on cattle. The Boobrie is rumored to live in the lochs of Argylishire.

- Bugbear - Is an English hobgoblin that looks like a bear.

- Buggane - Depicted as a huge ogre or troll, the Buggane is a creature that is native to the Isle of Man.

- Bwbachod - A Welsh household spirit said to be mischievous that detests people who don't drink alcohol.

- Cailleach Bheur - Said to be a blue faced hag, she is linked to winter and is a guardian to all animals.

- Cait-sith - Known in both Ireland and Scotland, this legend is that of a spectral cat that is said to possibly be a witch who can transform into a cat nine times.

- Ceasg - A Scottish mermaid who is half human, half salmon. If a Ceasg is captured, it is rumored that she will grant three wishes.

- Coliunn Gun Cheann - In folklore, this being was a large monster with no head who haunted the Macdonald lands near Morar House. Travelers would be found in the area mutilated by the creature until a clan member banished him.

- Cú-síth - A magical hound found within the folklore of Scotland that roams the moors. It is said to be the size of a small cow and has shaggy dark green hair. Should one hear the barking of the hound, they must reach safety by the third bark or they will be doomed.

- Dunters - These creatures stalked their prey near the old fortresses of the Borders. It is believed that they are the memory of foundation sacrifices.

- Fideal - This creature inhabited Loch Na Fideil near Gairloch and was said to drag women and children under the water to devour them.

- Fomorian - A supernatural race that comes from beneath the sea. They are enemies of the Tuatha Dé Danann with hostile attitudes. They are harmful and cause chaos, darkness, and death wherever they go.

- Morool - A sea monster from Shetland that is said to have many eyes.

- Nuckelavee - This creature had no skin so its muscles and vein structure could be seen. Described as a revolting part horse/part man creature.

- Urisk - These spirits are said to haunt pools and waterfalls and appear similar to a faun but are half human/half goat.

- Wulver - From the Shetlands, this supernatural being had the body of a man and the head of a wolf. Despite its frightening appearance, they were said to be benevolent.

Chapter 4: Celtic Magic and Spirituality

The Celts embraced their gods and goddesses along with the nature of the sacred land that they stood for. Each season had specific rituals that they followed throughout the year. They worshipped the sun and observed both lunar and solar cycles and applied these as reminders for planting and harvesting. The Celts were far more advanced than the simple hunter-gatherer societies that Shamanism typically springs from.

We have already mentioned that the Celts had a wide display of magic throughout their world and that nature was intricately woven throughout their history. They observed nature closely to reveal her secrets of both the metaphysical and the physical. They believed that Otherworlds that were supernatural in nature were close to their own, sharing borders that were easily crossed during significant magical times or circumstances.

The tales passed down from generation to generation reflect shamanic beliefs. The land was always revered by the Celts. They looked upon their land as a living, breathing, and sentient being who provided them with all their necessities. Their harvest was never looked at as an end, but a needed cycle to perpetuate the crops for the following year. Their people were often born, lived, and died in one spot, and when they passed away, they were buried in the land that cared for them over the years. It was here that they believed the spirit would be born anew.

The art of connection to the living land was a wisdom the Celts passed on, teaching those new generations how to understand seasonal changes, ley lines, and natural energies. Every living thing surrounding them was personified by a god or goddess, and every place, lake, or tree had a story.

The Celtic Bards were the keepers of the histories and were well known for their ability to memorize and retell the stories and songs of the Celtic culture that numbered in the hundreds.

Their myths were a valuable tool to the Celts, enabling them to understand natural occurrences. They believed that magic would bring fertility, and the Celtic shamans practiced their rituals within the walls of nature. These places of power were most likely on ley lines where there was an abundance of energy. Before any ritual, the shamans would call to their ancestral spirits and use animal totems to increase the magical forces and allow shamanic journeys.

Animal Totems

It was common for a Celtic god or goddess to also have an animal form or animal familiar. Since animals are also a part of nature, it only stands to reason that the Celts would also have magical ties to not only the creatures of the forest, but their spirits as well. These animals were often featured in Celtic jewelry, carvings, or pottery. The Celts believed that they held power and insight and were there to teach, guide, and make one a better person. Some of the prevalent creatures included:

- Wolves were always thought of as mystical creatures and were believed to be guides to the Otherworld.

- Bears were recognized as having king-like attributes.

- Different birds can carry symbols of messages, stand for symbols, and bring death or rebirth. For example, the goose represented change.

- Deer were considered magical creatures by the Celts. Their horns were a symbol of life force and recall how the Celts believed the soul was carried by the head. Deer always figured prominently in Celtic mythology because they were the supernatural messengers of the faerie world and often escorted people to the Otherworld.

- Foxes were known for their intelligence, but also for their playful side.

- The bull was a sign of male power and strength, but the bull can also create problems because of his stubbornness. In Celtic culture, women would place images of the bull in their homes as a symbol of fertility.

- Cats were the keepers of the Celtic Underworld known for their knowledge and wisdom.

- Dogs, as with most every culture, are the protectors of the family. Celts viewed the dog as a sign of good health and loyalty.

- The Celtic griffin is a part lion, part eagle mythical creature that provides both positive and negative attributes. The Celts believed the griffin to be a sign of power, justice, and nobility.

- A butterfly was the symbol of rebirth, inspiration, and transformation. Perhaps the butterfly was chosen for this because of its cocoon/emergent stage and how it parallels the Celts view of death providing a path to another life.

The Celts used shapeshifting as a way to connect with animals. The idea of shifting brings to mind a rebirth and many of the Celtic myths include creatures with the ability to shift.

Celtic shamans would prepare for a shape-shifting journey by disregarding the natural laws of gravity and perceptions while they became anything of their choosing. The shamans believed that they could strengthen their bond with their spirit animals by experiencing a completely different world through another's eyes. If they chose to become an eagle for example, the shaman would be able to observe the world from the sky and gain a new perspective. If they choose a wolf or deer, they could experience how it feels to be wild and free. They believed that when they changed their outer form, they gained inner perception, and with those changes, one could develop into a different and better person.

Celtic Festivals

The Celtic wheel of the year is their annual cycle of the festivals that they acknowledge and how it ties in with their myths, legends, and farming rituals. The observation of these passing seasons plays an important part in the Celtic ideals of rebirth.

Yule/Winter Solstice

The Winter Solstice has been marked as the most important celebration in the pre-Christian world and marks the shortest day and the longest night of the year. The Celts marked this

Solstice as a day each year where a battle takes place between the Oak King (representing the light), and the Holly King (representing the dark). The Oak King would emerge victorious every year, and daylight would slowly return, only to engage in battle again at the time of Summer Solstice.

Celtic priests were said to cut the mistletoe that had grown on oak trees and give the cuttings as a blessing.

Food shortages were common during the first few months of winter, so the Yule was the last celebration the Celts had before winter began. At this time, most of the cattle would be slaughtered so they did not have to be fed through the winter, which also offered them a supply of fresh meat for the festival.

Within the Druid traditions, it is said that the sites of Newgrange and Stonehenge align with the sunrise and sunset of the solstice. Practices delegated to this Midwinter fest include gift giving, feasting, and sacrificial offerings which may have included food, objects, and lives of animals or lives of humans. The Druidic priests were also the ones who supported the tradition of the yule log. According to the story of the Celtic people, it is said that during the middle of the winter, they believed that the sun stood still for twelve days. Sometime during these days, a yule log was lit using last year's fire. This practice was believed to banish evil spirits, conquer the darkness, and bring good luck for the next year.

The Celts had a tradition of decorating the Yule tree, something that most of us probably practice today. They used bright colored objects hung on the pine tree to represent objects which held importance for them. These items represented things like the stars, the moon, the sun, and things that represented the soul of a person that had died that year. They practiced gift giving as offerings to the gods and goddesses, and these gifts included imitation fruit as a symbol of fertility, dolls that stood for human sacrifice, and candles that were used in pagan solstice celebrations. Sometimes this tradition included picking a 'mock' king from a group of prisoners, and he was provided with anything he desired for the seven-day festival, culminating in him being killed at the end.

Imbolc

The Celtic pagans dedicated this festival to the goddess Brigid who was considered one of the most powerful Celtic gods and the daughter of Dagda. Imbolc is recognized as a time to let go of past concerns and look toward the future. It was a time to make new beginnings and spring clean your soul.

Also referred to as Candlemas, Imbolc is celebrated February 1st and 2nd, signaling the halfway point between the winter solstice and the spring equinox. The Celts were said to welcome Brigid into their homes by crafting images of the goddess from bundles of crops such as oats.

Practices for Imbolc include:

- Making Brigid Crosses - The original names for these were cros Bride or bofha Bride, and they were crafted on the eve of the feast day and hung in homes or stables.

- Make an effigy - Called a Brídgeóg, these represented Brigid, and groups of young people would go door to door with them. The materials used to build the effigy are a broom, churn stick, or sticks as the body. The head was made up of either a carved turnip, mask, or stuffed straw.

- Construct a crown of rushes - A chosen young woman wears a crown built of rushes and carries a woven shield and a veil.

- Put out the Brat Bhrighite - This is a practice where a silk ribbon referred to as the 'ribín Brighid' is placed on a windowsill to see if during the feast it would grow longer. If it is touched by Brigid, it absorbs her healing and vitality, allowing the owner to remedy headaches.

- Practice divination - No matter where one lives, they always look forward to better weather. The Celts practiced weather divinations if they, for example, saw hedgehogs coming out of their holes. This was an indication the Spring was coming sooner rather than later. If the hedgehogs returned, rain was expected shortly.

- Gather the Hoar Frost - A hoar frost that is gathered from the grass on feast day is a Celtic remedy for headaches. Owners provided special food to their animals because of Brigid's love of animals. In addition, the Celts would take water from one of the many wells dedicated to Brigid and sprinkle the water around the house, the family, the barn, cattle, and fields.

- Feasting - A self-explanatory practice in which the Celts would have a great feast in honor of Brigid.

- Putting butter out - A common practice to make Brigid feel welcome is to put out a piece of cake and butter on the windowsill outside. It didn't matter if a poor person ate it or it was brought in and eaten by the family; legend says Brigid had blessed it.

Spring Equinox

A celebration for the end of Winter and the beginning of Spring when the earth is reborn, and the daylight stays longer. Spring Equinox is a festival of planting and fertility, and the Celts practiced rituals focused on rebirth. Rabbits and decorated eggs both featured prominently in this celebration as traditional Celtic symbols. In Wales, they planted seeds on this day after all other rituals were observed.

The Celtic story of Tarvos tells of a golden bull reborn after his winter's sleep, signifying to everyone that it is time to wake from winter's deep slumber.

Beltane

An annual Celtic festival that is celebrated on May 1st marks the start of Summer. Beltane means fires of Bel, and besides being a fire festival, it celebrates the fertility of the coming year. The Celts believed that if they drove their livestock between two large fires it would protect them from disease.

Fire is the most important element of Beltane, and it is believed to cleanse and purify the community. Celts leaped over the fires of Beltane to revitalize themselves by bringing good fortune and happiness to their family for the coming year. The Celts would also carry rowan or oak branches three times in the direction of the sun's path around the flames of the Beltane bonfire which offered them protection from natural and supernatural forces and provided good fortune. When the bonfires had been reduced to embers, the people would sprinkle themselves, their crops, and their livestock with the ashes.

The Celts also prepared food at the bonfire and had rituals tied to the feast. A lamb was sacrificed and prepared for the feast. In addition, there was a form of oatmeal cake made from eggs, butter, oatmeal, and milk that was cooked on the bonfire. Those present at the feast would take a 'Beltane bannock' and offer some to the spirits to protect their livestock. Another piece was offered to each of the animals that might cause harm to their livestock.

Traditional dancing around the Maypole results in the crowning of the feast's King and Queen who then wear May flowers strung together in celebration.

During Beltane, the people would visit holy wells. A holy well is a small body of water that carries with it some status in a folklore tale from the area. The water is said to contain healing qualities, and the visitors would pray for health while walking east to west around the well.

The popularity of Beltane as a fest had suffered greatly, and by the mid-twentieth century it had mostly died out. There are some attempts to bring back the practice of Beltane, but for now, it is only a festival for Celtic Reconstructionists and Wiccans.

Summer Solstice

This fest is halfway through the growing season and was used as a time to pray for a good harvest. Summer Solstice was viewed as a time of nature and new beginnings but also a time to banish evil spirits.

The Celts believed that they must light bonfires to repel evil spirits that might bring harm to their crops, livestock, or family. The celebration was a time of singing, dancing, feasting, and bringing luck to a relationship.

Irish Celts would pray to Gráinne, who was the Winter Queen and Solar Sun goddess. The Druids also had their own name for Summer Solstice, Alban Hefin, meaning the light of Summer or the light of the shore.

During the Summer Solstice, the axis tilt of the earth is closest to the sun, so there are more hours of daylight than at any other time of the year.

This was also a magical time for the gathering of healing herbs.

- Fern seeds gathered at this time were said to make one invisible.
- Elderberries protected the gatherer against enchantment.
- Vervain and yarrow were hung in the home to protect against the evil eye and death.
- St. John's wort was said to bring prosperity to a home,

health to the inhabitants and their livestock, and an abundant harvest.

Gifts of desserts, milk, honey, and wine were left out for the fae to encourage the continuation of the relationship between them and the Celts.

Lughnasadh

At the beginning of August is the time for the Celtic people to celebrate the festival of the Irish god Lugh. At this time, the harvest begins and continues through the Autumn Equinox, right up to Samhain. This festival is also in celebration of the wedding feast of Lugh, the courageous warrior god and god of the setting sun, and for Rosemerta, the rose mother.

The foods for the feast include grain products like cakes and breads as well as fruits and vegetables. The celebration areas are decorated in harvest colors of yellow, brown, orange, rust, and gold.

Lughnasadh is a time when the forces of light and dark join, causing two portals to appear. One opens prior to sunset and the other immediately after the sun goes down. If it happened to rain during the festivities, the Celts believed that Lugh had joined them. At this particular celebration, horses were in abundance not only in celebration of Lugh's white horse, but also because the ground was usually dry enough to participate in horse racing.

Autumn Equinox

The Autumn Equinox is best known for being equal parts of day and night and is the final festival of the harvest season.

For Celts, this is a time of reflection for the past season, recognizing that Summer is over and the process for collecting seeds for the next growing cycle has begun.

Samhain

This is a very important celebration by the Pagan Celts as the feast of the dead.

At this time of year, the Celts believed that the veils between their world and the Otherworld were at their thinnest, allowing the spirits of the dead to mingle with the living. With the veils down, the Celts were convinced that the world was teeming with magic.

What most do not understand is that though this festival has death as a central theme, it is not meant to be gruesome. The Celts did not fear death, rather they saw it as a necessity of life and rebirth. Just as people of other faiths, the Celts showed honor and respect for their dead. If a family member had recently passed, their spirits were invited to join the living at the feast.

Samhain is a time of reflecting on mortality, the passing of friendships, and a time for coming to terms with the past so that one could move on to the future. It is a time of year when the families choose which animals would be kept for next year's breeding and which would be slaughtered to feed the family through the winter.

In celebration of Samhain, the Druids built huge bonfires while the people brought sacrificed animals and harvest foods to serve at the celebration.

Throughout the celebration, the Celts wore costumes and entertained each other while trying to read their fortunes. There was also a tradition called mumming and guising that involved participants traveling from house to house in costume while reciting songs or verses in exchange for food. This tradition may have evolved from an earlier tradition where people impersonated the souls of the dead.

At the end of the festival, they would light the fires in their individual homes to signify protection and warmth during the winter months to come.

Chapter 5: Modern Celtic Traditions

For thousands of years, the mysterious traditions of the Celts have intrigued and inspired other generations to adopt a few or more of their practices. The Celts themselves built or adapted many of their traditions because of their exposure to other cultures throughout history.

The word *Celtic* covers a lot of traditional ground today and has led to a Celtic revival filled with language, festivals, music, literature, and art. Even sports like hurling (an outdoor team game similar to Gaelic football), Gaelic football, and shinty (a team game played with sticks and a ball), are perceived as being Celtic.

There are many distinct styles of Celtic music, and their trademarks usually feature traditional instrumental music that can be thought of for dancing reels and jigs. If there are lyrics, they are usually in a narrative style that tells a story. There are seven instruments key to Celtic music, and they are: the fiddle, flute, tin whistle, bodhran (Irish drum), concertina, harp, and the Uillean Pipes (a set of seven pipes similar to the bagpipes). Probably the best known Celtic musical group is The Chieftains.

Origins of early Irish dancing seem to be lost to the march of time, but there seems to be some similarities between the early

Celtic dance and the modern Irish dance. We now see an evolution in the art of the dance as folk dancing has evolved into productions of Riverdance or Lord of the Dance. There are traditional Gaelic events held that provide opportunities for Irish dancing competitions, musical performances, and storytelling.

There still exist different types of Celtic groups that range from the pagan practice of magic, tribal festivals, or members of a small Druidic college. These groups are usually informal but practice the Celtic ways with a sense of tradition.

Along with these groups there has been a renewal of Celtic Wicca. Because of being so widespread, the Celtic Wicca can be difficult to define, but they seem to center on Welsh and English practices of elemental magic, Druidism, and the fae.

Whether they are from Ireland, Wales, Scotland, England, or elsewhere, they are all dedicated to the protection of the Earth and focusing on linking humanity with nature. The Celtic practitioners of today are interested in self-discovery and empowerment. They crave a better understanding of the universe and encourage artistic abilities.

These modern Celtic followers use the same wheel of the year and celebrate the eight solar festivals along with the phases of the moon. Celtic traditions about nature, animals, and spirituality draw in many kids and teens. Because there are no set rules regarding the practice of Celtic Wicca, it holds a large appeal for independent thinkers and people from all walks of life.

Rebirth is a basic teaching from the ancient roots of the Celts, and currently Celtic Wicca has also embraced that through the concept of each person carrying the memory of our ancestors within our DNA. In a way, this provides us with a past that we can reawaken.

Conclusion

The world of the Celts is a fascinating one. As you may have noticed, there are many similarities to current celebrations and traditions. It's true that cultures will create gods, goddesses, myths, and stories to explain the happenings in their world.

The Celts seemed overall to be a simple, down to earth people that cherished their land, animals, and family, and over the years produced many myths and legendary figures that still reside with us today. From historical deduction, we have determined that there was probably no large-scale Celtic invasion, but people who were likely there originally or had a steady flow of resettling into the areas they dominated before the Roman war.

Unfortunately, we will never know the answers to all of our questions unless we can climb into a time machine and visit the ancient Celts to discover all of their secrets. We can only take the stories of the Celts handed down from the Romans and construct our own conclusions from their information. Albeit they had their own agenda since they were at war with the Celts, and even professed confusion at the impressive list of over four hundred gods and goddesses they compiled from the different Celtic tribes.

You should now have an idea of who the Celts were, and understand how they were made up from many different tribes that were similar in many ways, but also very different in others.

Delving into their religion, we found that the Celts were religious with high morals, yet they had a touch of warrior within the farmers they evolved into. Each tribe had gods and goddesses that were recognized across the different nations, yet often that same god would go by several names. In addition, it seems that each region developed its own list of deities.

The Celts were rich in heroes, myths, dangerous creatures, and the magical fae. They believed in shamanism, the wheel of the year broken up by festivals, and their connection to the land and family. Their beliefs are what held their society together.

We have determined that the Celts did not just disappear but likely mingled with the rest of the populace based upon simple DNA evidence.

Thank you for taking the time to read this book. I hope you have enjoyed learning all about the Celtic people and their fascinating history, legends, and traditions!